MOSES
AND THE
BURNING BUSH

MOSES
AND THE
BURNING
BUSH

R.C. SPROUL

ℝ *Reformation Trust* A DIVISION OF LIGONIER MINISTRIES, ORLANDO, FL

Moses and the Burning Bush
© 2018 by R.C. Sproul

Published by Reformation Trust Publishing
a division of Ligonier Ministries
421 Ligonier Court, Sanford, FL 32771
Ligonier.org   ReformationTrust.com

Printed in York, Pennsylvania
Maple Press
0000319
First edition, second printing

978-1-56769-863-3 (Hardcover)
978-1-56769-916-6 (ePub)
978-1-56769-917-3 (Kindle)

Interior design and typeset: Katherine Lloyd, The DESK

Scripture quotations are from the ESV® Bible (The Holy Bible, English Standard Version®), copyright © 2001 by Crossway, a publishing ministry of Good News Publishers. Used by permission. All rights reserved.

Scripture quotations marked KJV are from the King James Version. Public domain.

Library of Congress Cataloging-in-Publication Data

Names: Sproul, R. C. (Robert Charles), 1939-2017 author.
Title: Moses and the burning bush / R.C. Sproul.
Description: Orlando, FL: Reformation Trust Publishing, 2018. | Includes bibliographical references.
Identifiers: LCCN 2017036641 (print) | LCCN 2017043110 (ebook) | ISBN 9781567699166 (ePub) | ISBN 9781567699173 (Kindle) | ISBN 9781567698633 (hardcover)
Subjects: LCSH: Moses (Biblical leader)
Classification: LCC BS580.M6 (ebook) | LCC BS580.M6 S67 2018 (print) | DDC 222/.1206--dc23
LC record available at https://lccn.loc.gov/2017036641

CONTENTS

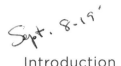

Introduction

A CONSUMING FIRE

righteous live—

The burning bush has been a significant symbol throughout the history of the church, and for good reason. In the account of Moses and the burning bush, we see God's self-revelation. God appeared to Moses and provided an all-important disclosure: His everlasting, covenant name, Yahweh. The burning bush, as a symbol, signifies an encounter with the transcendent God and His divine revelation.

The account of the burning bush is a story about the holiness of God. What happened at the burning bush was a *theophany*—a visible manifestation of the invisible God. Moses' attention was caught by something mysterious. He saw a bush that was burning but not consumed. As Moses drew near to the bush, God spoke, telling him, "Take your sandals off your feet, for the place on which you are standing is holy ground" (Ex. 3:5). The ground was holy not because of the presence of Moses but rather because of the presence of God. It was holy ground because at that point, an intersection between heaven and earth occurred. God Himself appeared, through the manifestation of His presence in the bush.

One of the church's biggest problems is that we don't understand who God is. But in that one revelation—the theophany in which God appeared to Moses—the transcendent majesty of God was partially unveiled. What had been invisible became visible through the theophany. Part of our problem is that when something is out of sight, it's out of mind. But from time to time throughout biblical history, God manifests Himself to human eyes. God manifested Himself at the burning bush, and it was earth-shattering.

We talk theologically about the transcendence of God and the immanence of God. On the one hand, God is not a part of the created order. He's above and beyond. That's what we mean by _transcendent_.

And yet He is not remote. Aristotle thought of God as a do-nothing king who reigns but doesn't rule. His god is uninvolved with the affairs of human beings. But God is not like that. He is *immanent*, meaning He is close by. He's immanent in that He manifests Himself in the created order. He's immanent through the presence of the Holy Spirit and ultimately by virtue of the incarnation of Christ.

Scripture describes God as an all-consuming fire, which refers to His transcendent majesty (Deut. 4:24; Heb. 12:29). But He entered into communion with His creatures in the garden of Eden. In that original fellowship, prior to the fall, Adam and Eve delighted when God walked in the cool of the evening. They couldn't wait to enjoy His presence. But after the fall, if there had been no grace from God, then there would have been only judgment, and we would be without hope.

The whole Bible is the story of God's stooping and condescending to His embarrassed, frightened, fugitive people who hide ourselves because we know that we are naked and are ashamed. And the first act of redemption in the Bible is that God stooped down and covered our first parents' shame (Gen. 3:21). He covered Adam and Eve's sin, fashioning for them tunics of animal skin.

The redemption motif from Genesis to Revelation is a covering. It's a covering because in our fallen condition we are naked before God. We're unclothed, and we require a covering that is acceptable to Him. By nature, other creatures have their covering that was provided by God. Birds have feathers. Other animals have their hides. But we need artificial covers and clothing. That in itself bears witness to our universal need for a covering. Even in the Old Testament sacrificial system, the throne of God in the Holy of Holies was covered with blood, which represented covering the sin of the people. The New Testament speaks of exchanging our filthy rags for the righteousness of Christ. The imagery we get in the New Testament is that we are covered, we are clothed, with the righteousness of Christ (Rom. 4:7–8; 2 Cor. 5:21).

Another familiar story in the Old Testament is Isaiah's vision of the Lord. Like Moses, Isaiah experienced the transcendence and immanence of the Lord:

> In the year that King Uzziah died I saw the Lord sitting upon a throne, high and lifted up; and the train of his robe filled the temple. Above him stood the seraphim. Each had six wings: with two he covered his face, and with two he covered his feet, and with two he flew. And one called to another and said:

"Holy, holy, holy is the LORD of hosts; the whole earth is full of his glory!"

And the foundations of the thresholds shook at the voice of him who called, and the house was filled with smoke. And I said: "Woe is me! For I am lost; for I am a man of unclean lips, and I dwell in the midst of a people of unclean lips; for my eyes have seen the King, the LORD of hosts!"

Then one of the seraphim flew to me, having in his hand a burning coal that he had taken with tongs from the altar. And he touched my mouth and said: "Behold, this has touched your lips; your guilt is taken away, and your sin atoned for." (Isa. 6:1–7)

Whether this vision occurred in the earthly temple or in the heavenly temple, one of the pieces of sacred furniture was the altar of incense. The altar of incense symbolized the prayers of God's people. And on the altar were coals, which God used to depict Isaiah's unholiness. When Isaiah saw God lifted up in His majesty, he immediately became aware of the dreadful contrast between himself and God. He cried out, "I am a man of unclean lips!" He cried out because his eyes had seen the Lord of hosts.

Isaiah realized who he truly was as soon as he realized who God is. He realized he was unclean. But we all, Isaiah realized, are filthy as well. And so to purify Isaiah for his mission, God dispatched a seraph to bring a burning coal from the altar and place it on Isaiah's lips. It wasn't for punishment; it was for purging. It was to make the unclean clean.

Just like Moses at the burning bush, Isaiah must have been terrified by his experience. Augustine said self-consciousness carries with it an immediate awareness of one's finitude. As soon as we are aware of ourselves, we know that we are not God and we know that we are subject to God. John Calvin said that we don't really understand who we are until we understand who God is; we don't first understand God until we encounter ourselves.

Calvin goes on to say that in our fallen condition we tend to think more highly of ourselves than we ought. We observe each other, and we judge ourselves according to earthly standards. We can always find someone who is more corrupt than we are, or at least who appears to be. But when we lift our gaze to heaven and consider who God is, then we are reduced to dread. We don't measure up to the standard He demands.

The Lord is holy, high and lifted up. He is a consuming

fire. And if not for His grace, we would be consumed. This is still true for us today: if not for the covering of Christ's righteousness, if not for the purging of our filthiness, we would be consumed. But God in His grace has condescended to make it possible for us to stand in His presence through Christ and live. What Moses experienced at the burning bush is what God's people experience today: a holy, transcendent, all-consuming God who comes down to dwell with His people. He knows us.

Chapter One

THE INVISIBLE HAND OF GOD

IN 1583, THE SYMBOL OF THE BURNING bush was first adapted for use as the official seal of the synods of the Reformed Church of France. Likely influenced by John Calvin's commentary on Acts 7:30—where he remarked that the church is in a constant state of subjection to the "fire of persecution," but, as Jesus promised in Matthew 16:18, the church is sustained by the presence of God and kept "from being consumed into ashes." Over the centuries that followed, the symbol or one like it was adopted by other branches and denominations of Reformed and Presbyterian traditions, including some that use it today.

That moment in biblical history when Moses encountered the presence of God in the burning bush is a watershed episode, not only for the life of Moses, or even for the history of Israel, but for the history of the entire world. This book will consider the significance of that event, looking at Moses' life leading up to that encounter and focusing on the knowledge of God that is revealed in that particular incident.

The account of the burning bush begins with an ominous statement early in the book of Exodus, which introduces a notion of profound concern that sets the stage for all that will follow in the book: "Now there arose a new king over Egypt, who did not know Joseph" (Ex. 1:8). Anyone who is familiar with the history that unfolded in the book of Genesis will immediately feel the weight of this statement. Genesis ends with the children of Israel being invited to move from Canaan, where severe famine had hit, into Egypt, where Joseph was serving as the prime minister. The Israelites were given the land of Goshen as a settling place, and as the years passed, the population of this group grew exponentially to become a large portion of the population of Egypt. In earlier days, they enjoyed the favor of the pharaoh who had promoted Joseph to the level of prime minister. But a new pharaoh came to power who "did not know Joseph."

That signals a radical shift in the relationship between

the Jewish immigrants and the host country of Egypt. This new king said to his people, "Behold, the people of Israel are too many and too mighty for us" (Ex. 1:9). That's probably hyperbole, but Pharaoh was very concerned about the growth of the Israelites in their midst. So he said, "Come, let us deal shrewdly with them, lest they multiply, and, if war breaks out, they join our enemies and fight against us and escape from the land" (v. 10).

Pharaoh had to be careful. He didn't want them to leave, because they were slave labor upon which the whole economy depended. At the same time, he didn't want them to become so numerous and strong that, if Egypt were attacked by another nation, there could be an insurrection. He needed to keep the Hebrew people in Egypt but ensure that they remained weak. So Pharaoh instituted a cunning plan: "Therefore they set taskmasters over them to afflict them with heavy burdens. They built for Pharaoh store cities, Pithom and Raamses. But the more they were oppressed, the more they multiplied and the more they spread abroad" (vv. 11–12). The idea was that the heavier their burdens during their period of slavery, the less likely they would live to old age; the life expectancy, particularly of the Hebrew men, would be shortened.

But the exact opposite result came to pass, and the

account says that the Egyptians "were in dread of the people of Israel. So they ruthlessly made the people of Israel work as slaves and made their lives bitter with hard service" (vv. 12–14). Pharaoh increased the burden.

What comes next bears enormous significance for the history of the world. But before we look at that, consider this question: Who was the most important person in the entire Old Testament? Some may say Adam. Some might suggest Eve, saying that she was the mother of us all. Others might nominate Abraham, the father of the faithful and the one whom God called into covenant with Himself. Some may suggest David, as the prefigurement of the King who would come in New Testament times in the person of Jesus. All of these are legitimate candidates.

I think the single most important person in the whole Old Testament is Moses, not only because he led the people out of bondage in the exodus but also because he was the mediator of the old covenant, just as Jesus is the Mediator of the new covenant. He is the one through whom God delivered the law to Israel in the form of the Ten Commandments. Without Moses' leadership, the Jewish slaves would not have been molded into a nation by God, and they would not have received the law delivered by Moses. Any study of jurisprudence in Western civilization reveals the impact of the Decalogue upon Roman, British, and American law. Moses is a man of enormous significance. We can see from the book of Exodus the extraordinary providence by which God, in His sovereignty, gave the world Moses.

Pharaoh's fear had escalated to such a degree that he created a new program to protect against the growing strength of the Jews: destroying the male babies that would be born. An edict came from Pharaoh, not unlike Herod's demand in New Testament days for the slaughter of newborn Jewish boys in order to destroy the Christ child: "Then the king of Egypt said to the Hebrew midwives, one of whom was named Shiphrah and the other Puah, 'When you serve as midwife to the Hebrew women and see them on the birthstool, if it is a son, you shall kill him, but if it is a daughter, she shall live'" (Ex. 1:15–16). This is not simply a government sanctioning abortion, as wicked as that is; it is a case where a government is commanding infanticide.

Then, in verse 17, we see that amazing biblical word: *but*. Something comes along that thwarts this decree of the most powerful ruler in the world. "But the midwives . . ."—who were surely intimidated by the power of Pharaoh—"But the midwives feared God." These were

God-fearing women who had more reverence for God and more fear of offending God than they had of offending Pharaoh. So, "the midwives feared God and did not do as the king of Egypt commanded them." Here is an act of civil disobedience that received the blessing of God. We are always to obey the civil magistrates, unless they command us to do something that God forbids, or forbid us from doing something that He commands. In this case, the midwives were commanded to kill these babies, which would violate the character of God and their own consciences—so they disobeyed Pharaoh; they "did not do as the king of Egypt commanded them, but let the male children live."

Pharaoh got word of this, and he called the midwives in, questioning them: "Why have you done this, and let the male children live?" (Ex. 1:18). How did the midwives respond? With a righteous lie.

There are such things as righteous lies. We understand the biblical ethic that there is a sanctity of truth, and we are to speak the truth whenever we possibly can. However, the principle is this: we are always to tell the truth to whom the truth is due. That is, we are always called to tell the truth, the whole truth, and nothing but the truth in the case of justice. However, if the enemy crosses your borders and wants to know where your company is bivouacked, you're not obligated to reveal that information. If a murderer comes to your house and wants to know where your child is and you know his intent is to kill him, you're not required by God to tell him, "He's hiding in the bedroom."

The midwives' action was a godly deceitfulness, and it received the full blessing of God. The midwives said to Pharaoh, "The Hebrew women are not like the Egyptian women, for they are vigorous and give birth before the midwife comes to them" (Ex. 1:19). Therefore, we are told, "God dealt well with the midwives" (Ex. 1:20). He blessed these women for their brave disobedience and dissent from Pharaoh's edict. "And the people multiplied and grew very strong. And because the midwives feared God, he gave them families. Then Pharaoh commanded all his people, 'Every son that is born to the Hebrews you shall cast into the Nile, but you shall let every daughter live'" (Ex. 1:20–22).

Next we read, "Now a man from the house of Levi went and took as his wife a Levite woman. The woman conceived and bore a son, and when she saw that he was a fine child, she hid him three months" (Ex. 2:1–2). You might be able to keep a six-week-old baby quiet, but by the time they are three months old, their cries cannot be silenced. People would begin to notice that an infant was nearby. "When she could hide him no longer, she took for him a basket made of bulrushes and daubed it with bitumen and pitch. She put the child in it and placed it among the reeds by the river bank" (Ex. 2:3). Interestingly, the Hebrew word for "basket" is the same word that is used for Noah's ark. She put him in a vessel, a little ark. She consigned her baby to the benevolence of God, to His sovereignty, and to His providence. She knew that she was no longer able to keep her baby safe. She trusted her God to save his life, protecting him from the wrath of Pharaoh. She didn't set it adrift in the Nile; she put it in the reeds, where it could still remain hidden, and had the baby's older sister watch to see if anyone would rescue the baby. In the providence of God, a woman came down to bathe at the river—and not just any woman; it was Pharaoh's daughter.

Imagine the terror in the heart of Moses' sister when she saw the daughter of Pharaoh approaching that small ark in the reeds that hid her baby brother. "She saw the basket among the reeds and sent her servant woman, and she took it. When she opened it, she saw the child, and behold, the baby was crying. She took pity on him and said, 'This is one of the Hebrews' children'" (Ex. 2:5–6).

She didn't just say, "This has to be one of the Hebrew babies. I'll report it to my father and have the soldiers come and dispense with this child." No. She had compassion. Her natural instinct, when she found a crying baby, was to pick that baby up and try to comfort him. Moses' quick-thinking sister spoke up: "'Shall I go and call you a nurse from the Hebrew women to nurse the child for you?' And Pharaoh's daughter said to her, 'Go.' So the girl went and called the child's mother. And Pharaoh's daughter said to her, 'Take this child away and nurse him for me, and I will give you your wages'" (Ex. 2:7–9).

"When the child grew older, she brought him to Pharaoh's daughter, and he became her son. She named him Moses, 'Because,' she said, 'I drew him out of the water'" (Ex. 2:10). This is how the life of Moses began. It was eighty years from that moment until Moses would meet the living God in the burning bush in the Midianite wilderness.

Chapter Two

THE BURNING BUSH

As we pick up the narrative that leads to the episode of the burning bush, we see what happened after Moses was adopted by the daughter of Pharaoh and brought into his house and family. In Exodus 2:11 we read, "One day, when Moses had grown up. . . ." That passes over an enormous amount of significant information; elsewhere in Scripture it says that, in the early years of Moses' development, he was raised as a prince of Egypt and given the most comprehensive and extensive education that was available anywhere in the world (see Acts 7:21–22). Again he was an example of extraordinary providence, in that he was given the opportunity of the best education that anyone could receive, all to prepare him to be not a prince in Egypt, but the mediator of the old covenant.

We read then, "When Moses had grown up, he went out to his people and looked on their burdens." So at some point he became aware that he was not an Egyptian by birth but was a Hebrew. This blood relationship to his kinsmen inclined him to see how they were faring. He "looked on their burdens, and he saw an Egyptian beating a Hebrew, one of his people. He looked this way and that, and seeing no one, he struck down the Egyptian and hid him in the sand. When he went out the next day, behold, two Hebrews were struggling together. And he said to the man in the wrong, 'Why do you strike your companion?'" (Ex. 2:11–13).

Moses here is trying to mediate a dispute between two slaves. He said to the aggressor in this fight, "Why are you doing this to your brother?" He replied, "Who made you a prince and judge over us? Who do you think you are, Moses? Do you intend to kill me like you killed the Egyptian yesterday?" Moses thought, "Oh, no. I thought I did that deed in secret, but the secret is out. This man knows I killed an Egyptian, and he knows where the body is buried."

This was the time for Moses to make haste and flee the jurisdiction of Egypt and seek safety elsewhere. So Moses said, "Surely the thing is known" (Ex. 2:14). "When Pharaoh heard of it, he sought to kill Moses. But Moses fled from Pharaoh and stayed in the land of Midian. And he sat down by a well" (v. 15). So Moses fled to Midian, in the desert, far away from the cities, and far from the hub of civilization.

What happened next reveals that Moses was a man whose heart was on fire for justice, with no patience whatsoever for seeing people abused and mistreated. "Now the priest of Midian had seven daughters, and they came and drew water and filled the troughs to water their father's flock. The shepherds came and drove them away, but Moses stood up and saved them, and watered their flock" (Ex. 2:16–17). This is masterful understatement: shepherds were chasing the women away, and Moses put a stop to it, defending them. We don't know how imposing a figure Moses was, but obviously these other fellows did not want to deal with him. This noble act eventually led to the situation in which, by happenstance of the hidden providence of God, Moses was adopted into a new family: the family of Reuel, who was the priest of Midian. Moses married his daughter Zipporah, had a son named Gershom, and found a home as a stranger in a foreign land.

"During those many days," we are told, "the king of

Egypt died, and the people of Israel groaned because of their slavery and cried out for help" (Ex. 2:23). Moses was forty years old. He was no longer a boy, but the same people who were subjected to the enormous burden of slavery imposed upon them by the Egyptians were still slaves. They were moaning and groaning as the burden of slavery became worse for them.

What happened in verses 23–25 is a significant moment in Old Testament history: "The people of Israel groaned because of their slavery and cried out for help. Their cry for rescue from slavery came up to God" (v. 23). God heard the cries of this people. In response, the Lord God, omnipotent, moved heaven and earth through His servant, Moses, to address that travesty of inhumanity.

"And God heard their groaning, and God remembered his covenant with Abraham, with Isaac, and with Jacob" (Ex. 2:24). God said to Himself, "These are the descendants of the man with whom I made a covenant, saying I would make him the father of a great nation and bless him, and that through him all the nations of the world would be blessed, and his descendants would be as the sand of the sea and as the stars of the sky. I repeated that promise to his son, Isaac, and then to his grandson, Jacob. I watched as their children went down into the land of

Moses

Egypt to the land of Goshen, but I've never forgotten that covenant promise that I made to Abraham and his descendants. Now I hear the sons and the daughters of Abraham, Isaac, and Jacob crying. Their cries are in My ears."

We read at the end of Exodus 2: "God saw the people of Israel—and God knew" (v. 25).

More years passed. Moses was eighty years old, and his job was to take the flocks of his father-in-law and have them graze to the edge of the desert, right to the base of Mount Horeb. For forty years, he had done this every single day. Moses was not enjoying the rank and privilege he previously held in the palace of Pharaoh; he was a shepherd, making sure the sheep were protected and fed day by day. It's hard to imagine a more boring existence than that.

When I was in high school, I worked in the summer at the Continental Can Company in Pittsburgh, which was one of the largest factories in the world. It produced cans of every type imaginable. Soup cans, Coke cans, grape juice cans, Delco battery fluid cans, and all the rest.

One of my jobs involved the old kind of bottle caps that you needed a church key to open. I would sit at a table with two huge bins. The bin on the left was filled with thousands of metal bottle caps. The bin on the right was filled with thousands of pieces of cork. I had to take a piece of the cork and push it into the base of the bottle cap, because that cork insulated the top of the bottle cap. Some people worked like that every day for eight hours. Some had been doing that same job for fifteen years. After fifteen minutes, I thought I was going to lose my mind.

Moses didn't complain that his work was humdrum. He did his monotonous job day in and day out, until one day he had the most incredible experience in all of his eighty years. We will dig into the theological significance of the narrative of this experience later. For now, let's refresh our memory of the narrative itself, which begins in Exodus 3.

"Now Moses was keeping the flock of his father-in-law, Jethro, the priest of Midian, and he led his flock to the west side of the wilderness and came to Horeb, the mountain of God. And the angel of the LORD appeared to him in a flame of fire out of the midst of a bush. He looked, and behold, the bush was burning, yet it was not consumed" (Ex. 3:1–2). Moses unexpectedly spied a phenomenon that he had never before witnessed: he saw a bush that appeared to be on fire, yet he noticed that in no way was the bush consumed. Notice his reaction. He said to himself, "I will turn aside to see this great sight, why the bush is not burned" (v. 3). That is, in essence, the subject of this book: to answer the question of why the bush was burning and yet not being consumed. The answer to that question, in a very real sense, opens the whole of redemptive history and encapsulates the very essence of God's self-revelation in history and in His Word.

"When the Lord saw that he turned aside to see, God called to him out of the bush, "Moses, Moses!" (Ex. 3:4). On top of the strange phenomenon of the bush that was burning and not being consumed, the bush then started talking to him, calling him by name. It used the repetition of his name, which was the Hebrew method of addressing someone in intimate terms of affection. 'Moses, Moses!' " and Moses said, "Here I am."

Then God said, "'Do not come near; take your sandals off your feet, for the place on which you are standing is holy ground.' And he said, 'I am the God of your father, the God of Abraham, the God of Isaac, and the God of Jacob.' And Moses hid his face, for he was afraid to look at God" (Ex. 3:5–6). Years later, when Moses went up on the mountain, he said to God, "Please show me your glory" (Ex. 33:18). But in this first encounter with the living God, he hid his face. He didn't dare look at what was right in front of him.

Then the LORD said, "I have surely seen the affliction of my people who are in Egypt and have heard their cry because of their taskmasters. I know their sufferings, and I have come down to deliver them out of the hand of the Egyptians and to bring them up out of that land to a good and broad land, a land flowing with milk and honey, to the place of the Canaanites, the Hittites, the Amorites, the Perizzites, the Hivites, and the Jebusites. And now, behold, the cry of the people of Israel has come to me, and I have also seen the oppression with which the Egyptians oppress them. Come, I will send you to Pharaoh that you may bring my people, the children of Israel, out of Egypt." (Ex. 3:7–10)

Moses had questions for God. His two questions in this encounter are of the utmost importance. The first is a question everyone should ask when in the presence of God: Who am I? "Who am I that I should go to Pharaoh and bring the children of Israel out of Egypt?" (Ex. 3:11). He must have been thinking, "It's one thing for me to stand up against a few shepherds out in the wilderness who are taking the water away from my father-in-law's daughters; it's one thing for me to stand up to an Egyptian who is beating one of the slaves—but who am I to go to Pharaoh and say 'Let my people go'?"

God answered: You are the one I will be with. "But I will be with you, and this shall be the sign for you, that I have sent you: when you have brought the people out of Egypt, you shall serve God on this mountain" (Ex. 3:12). Then Moses asked his second question: Who are you? "If I come to the people of Israel and say to them, 'The God of your fathers has sent me to you,' and they ask me, 'What is his name?' what shall I say to them?" (Ex. 3:13). God's response was profound:

> God said to Moses, "I AM WHO I AM." And he said, "Say this to the people of Israel: 'I AM has sent me to you.'" God also said to Moses, "Say this to the people of Israel: 'The LORD, the God of your fathers, the God of Abraham, the God of Isaac, and the God of Jacob, has sent me to you.' This is my name forever, and thus I am to be remembered throughout all generations." (Ex. 3:14–15)

In that self-disclosure is found a revelation of the nature and character of God that is as deep as any that can be found in sacred Scripture. The task in the chapters to come is to explore the significance of these things. What do they mean? Why the burning bush? Why the memorial name "I AM WHO I AM"? Who is this God who revealed Himself to Moses in that moment of history?

Chapter Three

THE GLORY
OF GOD

ACCORDING TO JEWISH TRADITION, the most common bushes in the area of the desert around Mount Horeb were bramble bushes. The assumption of Jewish historians was that the particular bush that Moses saw burning was a simple, ordinary bramble bush of no great significance in itself. So, the first thing we must understand is that before the burning bush event, there was nothing at all supernatural about the bush itself; it was a natural, common bramble bush doing what bramble bushes naturally do in the desert.

In describing the experience of the burning bush in Exodus 3, Moses uses phenomenological language; that is, he says what it looked like. He was walking with his sheep in the desert, he saw the strange phenomenon of a bush burning, and he turned aside to see what this was all about. He was astonished to see that, although the bush was burning, it was not consumed. What Moses saw was a fire *in* the bush; it wasn't beside the bush or on top of the bush like the flames and tongues of fire that came down on the day of Pentecost. From Moses' viewpoint, the fire was coming from within the bush. The significance of his comment that the bush was not being consumed indicates that the bush itself was not burning—the fire was *in* the bush, but not *of* the bush.

What is the significance of the fire's being in the bush but not of the bush? It indicates that the fire Moses saw was independent of the bush—it was not using the bush for its fuel. That's why the bush wasn't consumed. It was burning from its own power. It was self-generated. This is a biblical example of what we call *theophany*, meaning "God made manifest." The God whom we worship is a spirit. He is invisible, and His invisible substance cannot be seen by the human eye. But there are occasions in redemptive history where the invisible God makes Himself visible by some kind of manifestation. That is called a theophany, and it's what we see with the burning bush.

In theology, such an activity as this—a bush with fire burning within it, but not being consumed—is said to be *contra naturam*, meaning "against nature." It was not a natural phenomenon but a supernatural one. What Moses saw in this fire was a supernatural, visible manifestation of the glory of God.

The Bible sometimes speaks about the outward appearance of God's glory—what we call the shekinah glory. It is a refulgent glory radiating from the very being of God that is so powerful and majestic that it overwhelms anyone who comes into contact with it. Throughout redemptive history, at critical junctures, God manifested Himself to people through the shekinah glory, which was represented chiefly through some kind of fire. This chapter will consider some of those episodes, particularly in the Old Testament.

In Genesis 15, we find the record of God speaking to Abraham and promising that he would be the father of a great nation. Abraham had been called by God, and God told him, "I am your shield; your reward shall be very great" (Gen. 15:1). Abraham asked, "What will you give me, for I continue childless, and the heir of my house is Eliezer of Damascus?" (Gen. 15:2). Abraham was already one of the wealthiest men in the world, and all that he lacked was what seemed impossible for him to have: an heir from his own bloodline.

God said, "'This man shall not be your heir; your very own son shall be your heir.' And he brought him outside and said, 'Look toward heaven, and number the stars, if you are able to number them.' Then he said to him, 'So shall your offspring be'" (Gen. 15:4–5). We're told that Abraham believed God, and that his belief was accounted to him for righteousness. But even as God spelled out all these things that He was going to do for Abraham, Abraham had the same basic struggles that we all would have in a situation like that; so he said to God, "O Lord GOD, how am I to know that I shall possess it?" (Gen. 15:8).

I've had the experience where people will ask me to tell them my "life verse." Maybe you have been asked that as well. I'm not sure where this idea ever came from; in my view, the whole Bible is our life verse. But people ask for my life verse, and I'm a little bit mischievous when I tell them my verse: Genesis 15:17. Often what happens is that, sometime later, they come back and ask, "Did you make a mistake on this verse that you told me? I looked at what you said was your life verse, and I can't make any sense out of it."

That verse says, "When the sun had gone down and it was dark, behold, a smoking fire pot and a flaming torch passed between these pieces." If I'm ever locked in a prison in solitary confinement and can have only one verse in all of the Bible at my disposal, that's the verse I want. Genesis 15:17 tells of a garish and gory ritual in which God commanded Abraham to cut animals in half and place the halves opposite each other, forming a pathway in the middle. A dread came upon Abraham in a vision, and in the darkness, while he was asleep, Abraham saw "a smoking fire pot and a flaming torch passed between these pieces." This text describes the making of a covenant. In Hebrew, you would say someone "cut" a covenant with another, and that's what this ritual pictures. In revealing Himself as a torch and a smoking fire pot that passed between the animal pieces, God was communicating to Abraham, "Here's how you can know that I'm going to do what I say I'm going to do, Abraham. If I ever fail to keep my promise to you, may I be like these animals, cut in two. May the immutable God suffer a mutation and become temporal, the infinite become finite. I swear by My own being."

The author of Hebrews picked that message up in the New Testament when he wrote, "For when God made a promise to Abraham, since he had no one greater by whom to swear, he swore by himself" (Heb. 6:13). It was an oath demonstrated by the shekinah glory made visible to Abraham in the darkness of the night. It was an oath by fire. Abraham and Moses both had the experience of encountering the (shekinah) glory of God in a fire that changed their lives.

In the New Testament, we read in Acts 9 about the Apostle Paul's experience of conversion on the road to Damascus: "But Saul, still breathing threats and murder against the disciples of the Lord, went to the high priest and asked him for letters to the synagogues at Damascus, so that if he found any belonging to the Way, men or women, he might bring them bound to Jerusalem. Now as he went on his way, he approached Damascus, and suddenly a light from heaven shone around him" (Acts 9:1–3). When he later recalled this event before Agrippa, Paul described it as "a light from heaven, brighter than the sun, that shone around me and those who journeyed with me" (Acts 26:13).

"And falling to the ground, he heard a voice saying to him, 'Saul, Saul, why are you persecuting me?' And he said, 'Who are you, Lord?' And he said, 'I am Jesus, whom you are persecuting. But rise and enter the city, and you will be told what you are to do'" (Acts 9:4–6).

Don't miss the parallel: when God appeared to Moses, He called to him out of that burning bush by the repetition of his name, "Moses, Moses." Then, when the shekinah glory appeared to Saul of Tarsus, the voice came again out of that brilliant, effulgent glory, saying to him, "Saul, Saul, why are persecuting me?" This was the encounter that turned Paul's life upside down and made him the greatest Apostle of the biblical era. What happened? What did Paul encounter? He came face-to-face with the glory of God, the brilliant, resplendent beauty of the shekinah.

There are other places in Scripture where this takes place, but the one that most are familiar with accompanied the birth of Jesus. Strangely enough, the shekinah glory wasn't in the cave or the manger; it wasn't with Mary and Joseph. It appeared in the fields outside Bethlehem, where the shepherds were tending their sheep. Luke's narrative says that the glory of God shown around about them. I like the old translation, "And they were sore afraid" (Luke 2:9, KJV). They were so terrified that the angels had to calm them, saying, "Fear not" (Luke 2:10). The angel of the Lord came, accompanied by a visible display of the shekinah glory that would make anyone tremble. Nevertheless, they said, "Behold, I bring you good news of great joy that will be for all the people. For unto you is born this day in the city of David a Savior, who is Christ the Lord" (Luke 2:10–11).

This shekinah glory that changed Moses' life, Saul's life, Abraham's life, and even world history at Bethlehem is not just linked to God the Father; it is inseparably related to the second person of the Trinity. When God appears in theophany with the shekinah glory, it's not only God the Father appearing—ultimately, what is displayed is the glory inherent to God the Son from all eternity.

Thus, it's not so much *what* was in that bush, but *who* was in that bush—who it was who was speaking to Moses centuries before Moses would speak with Him on the Mount of Transfiguration, which was clearly the most magnificent display of the shekinah glory anywhere in the New Testament (Matt. 17:1–8). Just as that bush was burning from the inside and the bush itself was not burning, so in the transfigured Jesus, the glory that was displayed on the mountain was not a reflection but a glory that burst from His concealed deity—because where the shekinah is, God is.

Chapter Four

GOD COMES NEAR

I WAS A PHILOSOPHY MAJOR IN COLLEGE, and in my sophomore year my philosophy professor invited me to go to Westminster Theological Seminary in Philadelphia to attend a conference on Dutch philosopher Herman Dooyeweerd. The original faculty of Westminster Seminary that had left Princeton to start that school was still intact. Cornelius Van Til, John Murray, E.J. Young, Ned Stonehouse, and the other great stars of that faculty were there for that conference.

When I listened to the first session, the whole thing was so far over my head that I had no idea what was going on. I felt foolish and didn't want to open my mouth and reveal how foolish I actually was, so I kept my mouth shut. But then during a lunch break, I found myself sitting across from the professor of philosophy from the seminary, who said to me, "Young man, do you believe God is transcendent or immanent?" I nearly spit out the soup I was eating, because I didn't know what the words *transcendent* or *immanent* meant. My ignorance was completely exposed to this learned professor.

He had mercy on me and began to answer the question for me. "The answer to the question, is God transcendent or immanent? is yes, because He is both transcendent and immanent. His transcendence refers to that sense in which God is above and beyond the created order; it refers to His exalted majesty, the way in which He is 'other' or 'different' from all the things that He creates. At the same time, God is not a remote deity who exists somewhere east of the sun and west of the moon, but God makes Himself present with us. He is also immanent in His creation by virtue of His omnipresence. He's immanent historically through the person of Christ. He's also immanent through His visitation to this planet in redemptive history."

We see this combination of transcendence and immanence in the burning bush. The fire was a manifestation of the transcendent God, the Creator, which you don't normally find in bushes. He made Himself known by manifesting His presence in this world through visiting Moses in that encounter in the desert.

Within the broad category of theophany, there is a subcategory called "Christophany." This refers to a pre-incarnate manifestation of Christ; that is, it addresses the question of whether we find the second person of the Trinity anywhere manifested in the Old Testament. Biblical scholars point to several passages in the Old Testament that indicate the presence of Christophany.

Consider Genesis 14, which describes Abraham's brief encounter with a mysterious person named Melchizedek. Verses 18–20 say, "And Melchizedek king of Salem brought out bread and wine. (He was priest of God Most High.) And he blessed him and said, 'Blessed be Abram by God Most High, Possessor of heaven and earth; and blessed be God Most High, who has delivered your enemies into your hand!' And Abram gave him a tenth of everything." Melchizedek was very important to the author of the book of Hebrews, because the Bible teaches that Jesus is not only our King after the line of David, but He has now entered into the heavenly Holy of Holies as our Great High Priest (Heb. 5). So the question is, how can Jesus be both a king and a priest? The Davidic king has to come from the tribe of Judah. Jesus did come from the tribe of Judah. But the priests came from the tribe of Levi and Aaron, so we speak of the Levitical priesthood or the Aaronic priesthood—and since Jesus did not come from that line, questions arose as to how He could legitimately be called the Great High Priest of His people.

The author of Hebrews answers this question by showing that Jesus is a priest not of the Levitical order or of the Aaronic priesthood but after the order of Melchizedek—referring back to the passage in Genesis. There is no genealogy listed for Melchizedek, which raises the question, was he a real historical character of flesh and blood, or was something else happening here? His name means "king of righteousness," and he was called the king of Salem, which means "peace." So this mysterious person was known in the Old Testament as the king of righteousness and peace, and these are attributes that the New Testament applies to Jesus.

Abraham met this priest of the Most High God, received a blessing from him, and paid a tithe to him. The author of Hebrews made much of this: "It is beyond dispute that the inferior is blessed by the superior. In the one case tithes are received by mortal men, but in the other case, by one of whom it is testified that he lives" (Heb. 7:7–8). In Hebrew categories, it was plain that Melchizedek was greater than Abraham; the father is greater than the son, the son is greater than the grandson, and so on. So, the author of Hebrews reasoned, Levi was lesser than Abraham, lesser than Isaac, lesser than Jacob; and if Levi was subordinate to Abraham, and Abraham subordinate to Melchizedek, that means that Levi was subordinate to Melchizedek—so Melchizedek represents the greater priesthood. Some even think that Melchizedek was a preincarnate manifestation of the second person of the Trinity.

Another strange encounter took place in Joshua 5: "When Joshua was by Jericho, he lifted up his eyes and looked, and behold, a man was standing before him with his drawn sword in his hand. And Joshua went to him and said to him, 'Are you for us, or for our adversaries?'" (Josh. 5:13). Here appeared an apparently mighty warrior whom Joshua didn't know. He had no military intelligence of a warrior like this fighting for the opposing forces. When he saw this warrior, he said, "Who are you? Are you with us or our enemies?"

Notice how the answer came: no. Joshua must have thought, "No? You have to be either for us or for them. Who are you?" "And he said, 'No; but I am the commander of the army of the LORD. Now I have come'" (Josh. 5:14). What did Joshua do? "And Joshua fell on his face to the earth and worshiped and said to him, 'What does my lord say to his servant?' And the commander of the LORD's army said to Joshua, 'Take off your sandals from your feet, for the place where you are standing is holy.' And Joshua did so" (Josh. 5:14–15).

This was a Christophany—the second person of the Trinity appearing in history before the conquest of the Promised Land.

Likewise, in Daniel 3:19–25, we see another example:

Then Nebuchadnezzar was filled with fury, and the expression of his face was changed against Shadrach, Meshach, and Abednego. He ordered the furnace heated seven times more than it was usually heated. And he ordered some of the mighty men of his army to bind Shadrach, Meshach, and Abednego, and to cast them into the burning fiery furnace. Then these men were bound in their cloaks, their tunics, their hats, and their other garments, and they were thrown into the burning fiery furnace. Because the king's order was urgent and the furnace overheated, the flame of the fire killed those men who took up Shadrach, Meshach, and Abednego. And these three men, Shadrach, Meshach, and Abednego, fell bound into the burning fiery furnace.

Then King Nebuchadnezzar was astonished and rose up in haste. He declared to his counselors, "Did we not cast three men bound into the fire?" They answered and said to the king, "True, O king." He answered and said, "But I see four men unbound, walking in the midst of the fire, and they are not hurt; and the appearance of the fourth is like a son of the gods."

The second person of the Trinity came into the fire for His servants Shadrach, Meshach, and Abednego, protecting them from all harm.

These examples of Christophanies fit within the larger category of theophanies, where God manifests Himself visibly somehow. The burning bush is an early example of such manifestations, but it was not the last. Throughout the book of Exodus, God appeared again and again as He led the people of Israel through the wilderness, as a pillar of cloud by day and a pillar of fire by night. At the end of the book, after the construction of the tabernacle was completed, the glory of God descended into the tabernacle. When Elijah was taken into heaven in 2 Kings 2, a chariot of fire appears, which manifested the divine glory as a mobile throne. This idea appears again in Ezekiel 1, one of the most enigmatic chapters in the entire Bible, where the prophet has a vision of the mobile throne of God surrounded by the splendor of His glory.

We read again and again in the Bible of a brilliant, radiant light, a light so intense that it blinds people and causes fear and trembling to come upon them. But what causes this light? The glory of God comes from His inner being; the shekinah is the outward manifestation of the inward majesty of God. But where does the light come from? The author of Hebrews answered that question when he spoke of Christ: he described Christ as the brightness of God's glory (Heb. 1:3). Christ is the visible manifestation of the eternal glory of God; in His divine nature, Christ is the shekinah. He's the One who lit the light, giving fire and flame to the glory of God. That's an incredible thing. We could ponder the rest of our days and never get to the bottom of the depths of the reality that Christ is the brightness of God's glory. The logical conclusion would be: if there were no Christ, no second person of the Trinity, then there would be only darkness in God.

The philosopher Philo of Alexandria made a connection—not from a Christian viewpoint but a philosophical one—between the glory of God and the Greek concept of the *logos*. The *logos* was a transcendent principle that gave order, meaning, and purpose to the universe in Greek philosophy; Philo tied this concept of the *logos* to the shekinah. This is consistent with the New Testament, as the gospel of John says, "In the beginning was the Word [*logos*], and the Word was with God, and the Word was God. . . . In him was life, and the life was the light of men. The light shines in the darkness, and the darkness has not overcome it" (John 1:1, 4–5). The *logos* is the Godness of God, the very brightness of His glory.

Chapter Five

HOLY GROUND

THE FRENCH EXISTENTIAL PHILOSOPHER Jean-Paul Sartre was perhaps most famous for writing the play *No Exit*. In the last act, a group of people sit in a room without doors, gazing at each other and reducing one another to objects. Sartre concluded the play by saying, "Hell is other people."

Throughout his works, Sartre, an atheist, maintained that there is no exit for people from hellishness, and that this is because there is no access to God, to the sacred, or to transcendent reality. He described human beings as useless passions, and concluded that the ultimate description of our human condition is found in the word *nausea*. This, he said, is because we are chained—trapped in the here and now—and there is no escape from the trap. There is no door or window by which we can reach anything of eternal significance.

In the twentieth century, one of the greatest sociologists of religion in the world, Mircea Eliade, responded to Sartre's description of the human predicament by saying that yes, human beings are in a profane state—but not because there's no access to the holy, no way in which we can encounter that which is sacred; rather, in our fallen condition, we choose an existence that is profane.

Profanity, as the rejection of the sacred, marks our culture in every medium, and it continues to escalate year after year. We talk of profanity of speech, but that is only one expression of living in the realm of the profane. Eliade went on to say that as much as we seek to live in profanity, human life simply cannot live in total profanity. Ultimately, it's not that there is no access to God, but rather there is no escape from the sacred, because everywhere the sacred intrudes upon our culture and our world. This affirms what Scripture declares. In Isaiah 6, when the prophet had his vision of being called and sent as God's spokesman, the song of the angels in the presence of God rang out, "Holy, holy, holy is the LORD of hosts; *the whole earth is full of his glory!*" (Isa. 6:3).

There is a sharp antithesis between the radical secularism of people such as Sartre and the teaching of Scripture. Scripture reveals that the holy or the sacred is not in some hidden realm that only the most brilliant, elite thinkers can penetrate. On the contrary, the whole earth is filled with the glory of God. Why then do we have this sense of the profane? John Calvin answered that question by saying that the whole of creation is a glorious theater, manifesting so clearly the holiness of God, but we are blind to it with a willful blindness. We are like people who walk into a glorious theater wearing blindfolds. And we have put the blindfolds over our own eyes, lest we see the holy and the sacred—because there is nothing more terrifying to sinful creatures than to be exposed to the holy.

That's what is on display in this account: Moses saw a bush that was burning yet not consumed, and as he turned aside to look at it, he began to walk toward the bush. Suddenly, a voice came out of the bush, calling to him by name, saying, "Moses, Moses. Don't come any closer. Instead, take your shoes off, because you are standing on holy ground." What made it *holy* ground? There was nothing particularly sacred about the soil in the Midianite desert. Nothing intrinsically holy could be found in the dirt. Rather, what made that ground holy was the presence of God. Anything God touches receives, as it were, a radiation from His own transcendent majesty. What made that ground holy and different from an ordinary piece of land was that it became an intersection where the natural earth was touched by the supernatural presence of God himself. This is what is called a threshold: a spot that marks a place of transition—a border—in this case, between the natural and the supernatural. When Moses came near that border, God said, "No farther, Moses."

On the front of the bulletin at Saint Andrew's Chapel in Sanford, Fla., these words are printed: "We cross the threshold of the secular to the sacred, from the common to the uncommon, from the profane to the holy." The church's leadership wants people to understand that when they come into the sanctuary on Sunday morning, they're entering a place that is different from a movie theater, a civic meeting hall, or any other place they visit in the world. As soon as they walk in, they've made a transition. They're entering a holy space, because this is holy ground. The very architecture of our church was designed to communicate that idea to people: when they come into the building, they're crossing a threshold. This is not a place that experiences the triumph of the secular or the profane.

Much has been said about secularism and secularization. All that the term *secular* originally meant was "this world," in terms of a particular time. Secularism as an ideology teaches this too—there is the here and now, and that's all there is. There is no heaven; there is no realm of the eternal or the transcendent. Secularism is a commitment to the idea that you only go around once—that this world is all there is, and there is no more.

But when people walk in the door of Saint Andrew's Chapel—or any other gospel-teaching church, where the holy God is present—they step across the threshold from the secular into the realm of the sacred. That which is sacred is different; it has been set apart divinely by God. The sacred space is where God steps, acts, and moves. Christians gather together on the Sabbath day because God calls us to do so. He says, "This is the place where I will meet with my people on Sundays." That's why the New Testament teaches never to neglect the assembly of the saints (Heb. 10:25); we as human beings need, every week, to visit holy ground—to get away from the secular and step across the border into the sacred. It's a place where we move from the ordinary to the extraordinary, from the common to the uncommon, from the profane to the holy.

Remember, from the book of Genesis, the experience that Jacob had at Bethel: he went to sleep and had a vision of a ladder going up to heaven, with the angels of God ascending and descending on it. The account says, "And behold, the LORD stood above it and said, 'I am the LORD, the God of Abraham your father and the God of Isaac.'" (Gen. 28:13). Then we read, "Then Jacob awoke from his sleep and said, 'Surely the LORD is in this place, and I did not know it.' And he was afraid and said, 'How awesome is this place! This is none other than the house of God, and this is the gate of heaven'" (Gen. 28:16–17). He took the stone that he had used as a pillow, and he poured oil on the stone, consecrating that rock. He marked it as holy ground, because there the Lord God appeared to him in his dream.

What Jacob experienced in Bethel, and what we experience in the life of the church, is exactly what Moses experienced there in the wilderness. He came near to the sacred, stepped across the threshold, and God spoke to him, stopping him, and telling him to come no farther. Then God said to him, "'I am the God of your father, the God of Abraham, the God of Isaac, and the God of Jacob.' And Moses hid his face, for he was afraid to look at God." At first, he wanted to look, but when he got closer and realized where he was standing—and who was there—he thought, "I can't look."

A family once went on vacation to St. Louis, and one of the things they wanted to do was visit the Cathedral Basilica of St. Louis. Before they entered it, the teenage daughter was being silly, making jokes and remarks about what they were doing. Then they went through the front door, and as soon as they got into the sanctuary, that girl became completely silent. Her parents were watching, and they noticed the transformation that came over her countenance as she looked up at the vaulted ceilings and the Gothic arches, and as she saw the mosaic tiles depicting the history of redemption. She walked tentatively. Seeing something across the room, she asked, "Is it OK for me to walk over there?" She was overwhelmed by a sense of the presence of the holiness of God. That should be everyone's experience every time they walk into a church—because in doing so they are crossing a border, making a transition.

Moses hid his face as he made that transition. But that's not the end of the story; it's just the beginning.

Chapter Six

I AM: THE NAME OF GOD

EXODUS 3:7 CONTAINS THREE different verbs that tell us something profound about God. First, God says He had _seen_; "I have surely seen the affliction of my people." God sees what's going on. Next God says He had _heard_; "and have heard their cry." Thus, we know that the God revealed here is neither blind nor deaf—and neither is He ignorant, because finally He said that He _knew_: "I know their sufferings."

Then from the burning bush God announced to Moses the purpose of this divine visitation: "I have come down to deliver them out of the hand of the Egyptians and to bring them up out of that land to a good and broad land, a land flowing with milk and honey. . . . Come, I will send you to Pharaoh that you may bring my people, the children of Israel, out of Egypt" (Ex. 3:8, 10). The first response Moses had was the question: Who am I? He said, "Who am I that I should go to Pharaoh and bring the children of Israel out of Egypt?" (Ex. 3:11). So the first thing that happened in Moses' encounter with God was that he became confused about his own identity. He suddenly doesn't know who he is. John Calvin began the *Institutes of the Christian Religion* by saying, in effect, "We never know who we are until we first know who God is."

Remember that the prophet Isaiah, after seeing God high and lifted up and hearing the angelic chorus cry, "Holy, holy, holy," responded by pronouncing a curse upon himself: "Woe is me! For I am lost; for I am a man of unclean lips, and I dwell in the midst of a people of unclean lips" (Isa. 6:5). For the first time in his life, Isaiah found out who God was—and at the same time, for the first time in his life, he found out who Isaiah was. That's what Calvin meant; he said that if we look at ourselves only in comparison to other people around us, soon we'll have such an inflated view of our own greatness that we will think of ourselves as only slightly less than demigods. But if, by chance, we lift our eyes to heaven, we will see the brightness of the sun—into which we cannot gaze directly, for it would destroy us. If we were to consider what kind of a being God is, we would tremble, being aware of our feet of clay and our frames of dust.

Moses had a momentary encounter with the Holy, and the closer he got, the more afraid he became. He heard the voice of God sending him on a mission, and his fear turned to doubt. "Who am I, that I should go on this mission?" And God responded, "I will be with you" (Ex. 3:12). He didn't really answer Moses' question about who Moses was; He simply said, in effect, "Don't worry about who you are, because I'm going to be with you."

"'And this shall be the sign for you, that I have sent you: when you have brought the people out of Egypt, you shall serve God on this mountain.' Then Moses said to God, 'If I come to the people of Israel and say to them, "The God of your fathers has sent me to you," and they ask me, "What is his name?" what shall I say to them?'" (Ex. 3:12–13). Now we get to the crux of the matter. Moses no longer was asking the question, "Who am I?" At this point, what Moses asked was, "Who are you? What's your name?"

In the very early days of Ligonier Ministries, somebody asked me, "What are you trying to do? What's your mission? What's the purpose of this ministry that you've put together?" I told him, "It's a teaching ministry to help ground Christians in the Word of God," and he responded, "What is it that you want to teach, that the people don't already know?" That was easy. "Who God is," I said. "Romans 1:18–25 tells us that everyone in the world knows *that* God is, because God has so clearly manifested Himself to all of them in creation that men are left without excuse, because His general revelation has pierced their minds. They know He exists, but they hate Him." I went on: "In large measure, that's because they know He is, but they don't have any idea *who* He is." The fellow said, "But what do you think is the most important thing that Christians need to know in this day and age?" I said, "Christians need to find out who God is."

I think the greatest weakness in our day is the virtual eclipse of the character of God, even within our churches. A woman with a Ph.D. in psychology who was a member of a church on the West Coast once got in contact with me. She was very angry and said, "I go to church every Sunday, and I get the feeling that our minister is doing everything he can to conceal from us the character of God. He's afraid that if he really opened up the Scriptures and proclaimed the character of God as He is portrayed in the Bible, people would leave the church because they would be uncomfortable in the presence of the Holy." Moses wasn't the first person to hide his face in the presence of God. That started in the garden of Eden, with the flight into hiding by Adam and Eve, who were ashamed.

So Moses asked, "Who are you? What's your name— if you even have a name?" God had already revealed Himself as "the God of your fathers, Abraham, Isaac, and Jacob" (see Ex. 3:6). Moses knew that; he wanted to know God's *name*.

In 1963, on national television, David Frost interviewed Madalyn Murray O'Hair, the famous militant atheist. Frost debated with O'Hair about the existence of God. As she was getting angrier and more frustrated, Frost decided to settle the debate in the classic American way: by taking a vote. He put it to the studio audience, saying, in effect, "How many of you people out there [about thirty people were there] believe in some kind of God, some kind of higher power, something greater than yourself?" Everyone raised their hands. O'Hair essentially responded, "What do you expect from the uneducated masses? These people haven't grown out of their intellectual infancy; they're still brainwashed from the culture and this mythology of God." She went on insulting everybody in the studio audience.

That's not what I expected her to do. I thought she would turn to the audience and say, "You believe in some kind of higher power, in something greater than yourself. Let me ask you: How many of you believe in Yahweh, the God of the Bible? The God who demands that you have no other gods in front of Him? The God who sends men, women, and children to hell forever, and condemns people because they don't believe in this mythical Jesus?" I wonder how the vote would have changed if the question had been asked with more clarity. It's almost an institution in our culture to describe God as a higher power, a force, something greater than ourselves. But what is that higher power? Gravity? Lightning? Earthquakes?

The trouble with a nebulous, nameless, characterless power is that, first, it is impersonal, and second and more importantly, it is amoral. There's an upside and a downside to worshiping such a higher power. The upside, to a sinner, is that an impersonal, amoral force makes no ethical demands on anyone. Gravity does not make judgment about people's behavior; even if someone should jump out of a window six stories high, there is no personal condemnation from gravity. No one's conscience is seared by gravity. If your higher power is impersonal and amoral, that gives you a license to behave any way you want with impunity.

The downside, however, is that there is nobody home. This belief means that there is no personal God, no Redeemer. What kind of a salvific relationship can you have with thunder? Thunder makes noise, booming through the sky—but in terms of content, it's mute. There is no revelation, no hope offered. Thunder and gravity have never been able to forgive any sin.

In God's answer to Moses, we see a contrast to this impersonal force. He didn't say, "It is what it is," which seems to be the name of false gods of our day. He said, "I AM WHO I AM" (Ex. 3:14). This name is related to God's personal name, *Yahweh*. So the very first thing that God reveals about Himself in that name is that He is personal. He can see; He can hear; He can know; He can speak. He can relate to the creatures He made in His own image. He is the God who brought up His people out of the land of Egypt. He is a God with a name and a history.

Many years ago, I taught a college course on theology, and we were studying the names of God. I was trying to illustrate the significance of the names of God, and what they reveal about God's character. Just before class, a girl, whom I'll call Mary, walked into the room in a strange, somewhat awkward manner—so that anyone could see the glittering diamond ring on her left hand. I said, "Mary, are you engaged?" She pointed to a man in the back room and said, "Yes, to John." I said, "Congratulations. When you say you're going to marry him, I assume you love him—is that a safe assumption?" She said, "Yes."

I said, "Why do you love him?" She said, "Because he's so handsome." I said, "Yes, he is very good looking. But look at Bill—he was the escort to the homecoming queen this year. Don't you think he's good looking?" She said, "Yes, Bill's very handsome." I said, "There must be something else about John, besides the fact that he's handsome." She said, "He's also athletic." I said, "Yes, he's good. But Bill's the captain of the basketball team. Why don't you love Bill instead of John?" She was starting to get frustrated, and said, "John's so intelligent." I said, "He is a very good student. Of course, Bill is probably going to be the valedictorian of the class. So, Mary, there has to be something else about John that distinguishes him from Bill in your eyes—something unique to him, that causes you to have this great affection. What is it about him that makes you love him so much?"

She became almost upset and said, "I love him because . . . I love him because—I love him because he's John." And I said, "There you go. When you want to focus on the crystalized essence of who he is, and what he means in terms of your relationship and personal history with him, it all comes back to his name."

I turned to the class and explained, "That's why, when we look at God, we know His name is wonderful. In that name, He reveals manifold things about the excellency of His being and the perfections of His character. And that's why the saints of old, if we asked, 'Tell us everything you know about God,' they would finally say, 'Yahweh—I AM WHO I AM.'"

Chapter Seven

I AM: THE BEING OF GOD

IN BIBLICAL TIMES, AND IN THE OLD Testament particularly, the names people were given revealed something about who they were. God renamed Abram "Abraham," saying, "For I have made you the father of a multitude of nations" (Gen. 17:5). Isaac, which means "laughter," was so named because, as Sarah said, "God has made laughter for me; everyone who hears will laugh over me" (Gen. 21:6). Jacob was renamed "Israel" because he wrestled with God. "Moses," as we discussed earlier, was significant because he was drawn out of the water.

Throughout the Scriptures, the names of individuals tell us something significant about their being or character. Nowhere is that more profoundly true than in Exodus

3, when God revealed Himself in an extraordinary manner by saying, "'I AM WHO I AM.' And he said, 'Say this to the people of Israel: "I AM has sent me to you."' God also said to Moses, 'Say this to the people of Israel: "The LORD, the God of your fathers, the God of Abraham, the God of Isaac, and the God of Jacob, has sent me to you." This is my name forever, and thus I am to be remembered throughout all generations'" (Ex. 3:14–15).

When critics read this account and see that God answered Moses in this strange and mysterious way by saying, "I AM WHO I AM," they conclude that God basically refused to reveal His name. They say that God in effect told Moses: "It's none of your business what My name is. I am who I am, and we'll let it go at that." But the context forbids that interpretation, because God made it clear that He was not refusing to reveal His name but that He in fact revealed His name to Moses—the name that is to be His name forever, for all generations.

Consider this simple question: Why does someone worship God? Why give to Him reverence and adoration that is different from any esteem that might be given to anything in the created world? It's easy to love God, be grateful to Him, and worship Him because of the wonderful things He's done in history, and in our own personal histories—but a Christian's reverence for God doesn't rise to true worship until that Christian worships God not for what He has done but for who He is in His transcendent majesty.

The theologians of the past said that God is the "most perfect being." We might quibble a bit with that description of God because, strictly speaking, perfection does not admit to degrees. But the church fathers wanted to get our attention with this intentional redundancy lest we underestimate the significance of God's perfection. All that He is, all of His attributes—His omniscience, omnipresence, eternality, and simplicity—are without blemish; they are free from any mixture of imperfection.

Let's now consider one of the oldest questions that philosophers, scientists, and others have asked. It's a provocative question, yet in its expression it is rather simple: Why is there something rather than nothing? In other words, why does anything exist in this universe? Without understanding the immensity of the galaxies and having no knowledge of the billions of unobservable stars that astronomers today tell us of—in his naked observation of the world around him, the psalmist said, "When I look at your heavens, the work of your fingers, the moon and the stars, which you have set in place, what is man that you are mindful of him, and the son of man that you care for him?" (Ps. 8:3–4). Even from the perspective of antiquity, the immensity of the universe overwhelmed him and made him feel utterly insignificant in the light of the vastness of reality as he perceived it.

Of course, when David penned those words, he didn't have a clue to the extent of the universe, even as we today don't really grasp the magnificence and immensity of it. The nearest star, of those billions of stars, is our own sun, which is ninety-three million miles away. To consider how far the next star is—let alone the furthest—is incomprehensible. Yet, the question arises in our minds: Why is there something rather than nothing? Why isn't the entire universe just empty space with nothing in it at all?

The answer is easy. It is so simple that it should never incite any kind of debate or argument. That answer is found in the first verse of the Bible, where we read, "In the beginning, God created the heavens and the earth" (Gen. 1:1). What we learn from this opening statement in Scripture is that there was a beginning; there was a time when all of these stars, trees, fish, animals, and people did not exist. Everything in creation has a beginning. Creation began at a particular moment in space and time. Before that, all that existed was God. Not nothingness, but God.

At the very beginning, there was God, and the beginning came to pass because this eternal God created everything.

People frequently inquire about and debate the origins of the universe. They posit theories on the subject of cosmogony, that is, how the universe came to be. The big bang theory is the most popular of these theories, and a simple explanation of it is that at one point in time, all matter and energy in the universe were compressed into an infinitely small "point of singularity." This point existed in a compressed state from all eternity; since eternity past, it had obeyed the law of inertia, which says that those things that are at rest remain at rest and things that are in motion remain in motion, unless acted upon by an outside force. The secularists say that we have an origin of the universe that defied the law of inertia, because for all eternity, this point of singularity remained in this organized state without mutation or change. But then one day it exploded—and the repercussions of that explosion are still being seen in the vastness of the universe, as the present universe seems to be expanding from that original explosion.

In a conversation with Carl Sagan about this, he said to me, "We can go all the way back to the first nanosecond before the big bang." I said, "Why do you stop there?"

He said, "We don't need to go back before that." I said, "There's nothing more plain than that need to go back there. If you're a scientist, you have to ask: 'Why the big bang? How did it occur? And what was before it?'"

What was before the big bang was a manifestation of the verb "to be." God did not say to Moses, "My name is 'Once upon a time, I Was. Now I Am, and I also have a future.'" That's not how God introduced himself to Moses. He introduced himself in terms of the eternal present. "I AM WHO I AM. I am the personification of the verb 'to be.'"

Philosophers of the ancient world sought to figure out how the universe came into being and how it could be understood in an intelligible way. Plato wanted to save the phenomena; that is, he thought that we ought to consider the experiences of all things we see and observe—birds, trees, crickets, and daffodils. How can anyone make sense of them? How does that diversity fit together in any coherent, meaningful whole? Parmenides said that the most important thing to understand is that whatever is, is. Nothing can exist apart from pure being, that is, being without change. He was challenged by Heraclitus, who argued that everything that we investigate in the world has one thing in common. Bears might differ radically from daffodils, but everything has something in common: everything in the world is in a state of becoming. He summed this up famously by saying that one cannot step into the same river twice. Everything is in a state of flux. In other words, you might put one foot in a river and wet your toes. Then you put your other foot in the water, but the river has moved on. It has changed. And not only that—you have changed.

One day, my wife, Vesta, brought out photographs from the first forty years of Ligonier Ministries, and there were many photographs of me. The naked eye could perceive the radical changes that had occurred over those forty years. Today I'm different from what I was yesterday, if only one day older, one hair grayer, one molecule weaker, one step closer to my own demise. What is true of me is true of everyone. The one element that everything has in common with every other thing is change. Every four years, during the election for the president of the United States, at least one candidate runs his campaign on the promise of bringing change. The assumption is that any change will be a good one, but that's not always the case. Things don't always change for the better.

Humans are creatures of change—and that's a key difference between humans and God. We distinguish between

God as the supreme being and us as human beings, so it appears that the difference between God and us has to do with the adjectives that qualify the concept of "being." He is supreme; we are human. But the real difference between God and humankind is *being*. He alone has being in and of Himself; He alone has eternal being. Any being that anyone or anything possesses is transitory and dependent; it's contingent, derived, a subset of pure being. That's what the Apostle Paul said to the Athenian philosophers with respect to God: "In him we live and move and have our being" (Acts 17:28).

To put it another way: without God, we couldn't live; our existence would be static, inert. The stars would freeze in their courses, because their motion is not independent. Aristotle understood that. For anything to move in this world, it has to be moved by something other than itself, which he called the "Prime Mover." Even our motion depends on the being of God. In Him, we live and move and have our being.

A common debate is how—or whether—the existence of God can be proven. If we define God as an eternal being from whom all things come and upon whom all things are dependent, that proposition can be proven, indubitably and compellingly, in about ten seconds, without having to jump into an abyss of darkness and embrace God with a leap of faith. It's rationally compelling. If there was ever a time when there was purely nothing, what could there possibly be now? Nothing. If anything exists, then something somewhere, somehow must have the power of being in itself. Without that, nothing can exist.

Chapter Eight

I AM: THE ASEITY OF GOD

WHEN GOD REVEALED HIS NAME "I AM" to Moses at the burning bush, He was revealing something very important about Himself, namely, that He is self-existent; He has the power of being in and of Himself. He depends on nothing and no one for His existence. This fact has enormous consequences for how we understand the world around us.

Antony Flew was an English philosopher who, though known for his work in philosophy of religion, was a devout atheist for much of his professional career. In fact, in 1968, he published a book titled *Reason and Responsibility*, which contained an argument against the existence of God. His argument became known as "Flew's

Parable." But at the age of eighty-one, Flew "converted" and became a theist, at one point saying, "I now real-ise that I have made a fool of myself by believing that there were no presentable theories of the development of inanimate matter up to the first living creature capable of reproduction."[1] Flew understood that, apart from this view, known as the "God hypothesis," science itself would be impossible.

The Christian faith is constantly under attack in the secular world, and in recent generations the weapons of criticism have been aimed chiefly at the idea of creation. Secularists understand that if they can refute the biblical concept of creation, they will have dealt a mortal blow against Christianity—and against all religion. Critics are cynical about the idea that the universe was created by God, a personal, transcendent, immutable being, saying that such an idea is unscientific, illogical, and a myth.

To understand the seeds of this skepticism, one must go back to the eighteenth-century Enlightenment. The principal thesis of the Enlightenment was that the God hypothesis was no longer necessary for modern science to account for the origin of human life or the universe. Before the Enlightenment, philosophers, even if they were not believers, had to give obeisance to Christian philosophy because they couldn't account for the universe apart from some idea of a transcendent being.

With the advent of the Enlightenment, all of this fell away. Scholars said, "We can explain the universe, and life in its origin, without an appeal to a transcendent deity." Some publicly declared themselves the personal enemies of God, saying they had identified the cause of the universe and of life: spontaneous generation. For instance, they would look at a mud puddle. With the naked eye, they could see nothing in the mud puddles, but then all of a sudden, tadpoles were swimming in the mud puddle. These scholars surmised that the tadpoles came into being through their own power. That is, they were self-created. (Today we would know that there were microscopic frogs' eggs in the puddle.)

There are only three possible explanations for anything that exists now: it is self-created, it is eternal, or it is created by something that is eternal. I gave a presentation at Yale, with faculty philosophers present, where I presented these options; they agreed that it had to be one of these three. Notice that the second two possibilities involve something eternal. If the first possibility can be eliminated, then the thesis that something has always been is proven.

Of course, the concept of spontaneous generation is simply another term for self-creation; it gets a lot of credibility in modern society, but careful examination of the concept will reveal that the idea is an absurd logical impossibility. Why? Because for something to create itself, it would have to be before it was—it would have to be and not be at the same time and in the same relationship, which violates a fundamental principle of truth and science: the law of noncontradiction.

When the Hubble Space Telescope was sent into space to gather more information on the expanding universe, one of the most famous astrophysicists in America was interviewed on the radio. He said, "Fifteen to seventeen billion years ago, the universe exploded into being." What was it before it exploded into being? The only option was nonbeing—which would mean that a fundamental scientific precept was violated: *ex nihilo nihil fit*—"out of nothing, nothing comes." When an otherwise distinguished astrophysicist declares that you get something out of nothing, he stops being a reputable astrophysicist.

In chapter 5, we briefly looked at French existential philosopher Jean-Paul Sartre and his play *No Exit*. Sartre also wrote a book titled *Being and Nothingness*. In that book, Sartre argued that if God exists, then morality is impossible—because for morality to be significant, people have to be not only free but autonomous. If God exists, we could not be autonomous; since we can't be autonomous, we can't really be moral. Thus, Sartre claimed, the existence of morality makes the God hypothesis impossible.

In the final analysis, the question of God's existence is really not an intellectual question but a moral one. Fallen human beings will go to every extreme possible to banish God as their judge. The controversy about intelligent design is about the same thing. "Intelligent design" is redundant; if something is designed, it had to have been by something intelligent. But we want to have unintelligible design—unintentional intentionality, and the absurdities mount up forever. The idea of self-creation is an attempt to explain the universe that is like pulling a rabbit out of the hat, but there's no rabbit in the hat until the magician waves his magic wand; then, voilà! Out comes the rabbit. But what this idea really posits is a rabbit out of the hat without the rabbit, without the hat, and without the magician.

In contrast to self-creation there is the idea of self-existence, or what is called in theology the concept of *aseity*. That is an obscure and esoteric term. Yet, that one little word captures all of the glory of the perfection of God's being. What makes God different from people, from the stars, from earthquakes, and from any other creaturely thing is that God—and God alone—has aseity; He alone exists by His own power. No one made Him or caused Him. He exists in and of Himself. This is a quality that no creature shares. People are not self-existent; neither are cars or stars. Only God has the concept of self-existence.

Some people stumble over the idea of God's self-existence—even someone like the brilliant twentieth-century philosopher Bertrand Russell. In his book *Why I Am Not a Christian*, Russell said that when he was eighteen years old, he read an essay by the philosopher John Stuart Mill. Up to that point, he had affirmed the existence of God. But, Russell said, "At the age of eighteen, I read John Stuart Mill's Autobiography, and I there found this sentence: 'My father taught me that the question "Who made me?" cannot be answered, since it immediately suggests the further question "Who made god?"' That very simple sentence showed me, as I still think, the fallacy in the argument of the First Cause. If everything must have a cause, then God must have a cause."[2] Russell had made an elementary error. The law of causality does not say that everything has to have a cause; rather, it says that every *effect* must have an antecedent cause. An effect is something that is caused by something else. A cause can only be a cause if it produces an effect. But God is not an effect, caused by something before Him. He is self-existent. He owes His being to nothing outside of Himself. He has the power of being within Himself.

Someone may ask, "What's the difference between self-creation and self-existence? Aren't they both a challenge to logic?" No—self-creation is illogical and absurd. But consider the idea of something that exists eternally on its own power. Is there anything irrational about that? That's not to say that if something can pass the test of rationality, it must be true. I'm not saying that. But the idea of self-existence violates no law of reason; it's a rational concept. Not only is the idea of a self-existent being possible, but as Thomas Aquinas said, "God's being, unlike any other thing that exists, is necessary being."

A necessary being is a being who cannot *not* be. It exists by the sheer necessity of its eternal being, of its aseity. A self-existent being is not hypothetical or dependent on another concept; it's necessary. God can't not be. Not only is God's being necessary ontologically, but it's also logically necessary. If anything exists now, something must have aseity. God must have the power of being within Himself that is not derived from something outside of Himself. This is transcendent being.

When we talk about God's transcendence, we mean that way in which God is greater and superior to anything in the finite, created world. Something has to be eternal, and if it is eternal, it is so because it can't stop being. But why can't there be some inanimate thing in the universe from which everything else derives? Why do we have to say that we need a transcendent being?

When we use the word *transcendent* with respect to God, we are not referring to geography, to where God lives. If God is self-existent, eternal, and pure, then He is, by definition, transcendent. He's a higher order of being. It is for that reason that God calls Himself "I AM." When we consider the transcendence and aseity of our God, we will respond in worship and awe—just as Moses did at the burning bush.

Chapter Nine

A DIVINE MISSION

MOSES WAS EIGHTY YEARS OLD AS he traversed the Midianite desert. He was a normal human being. He may have been asking himself, "Why am I here? Is my life just a waste of time? All that training I received in Pharaoh's house, the education that I was given in Egypt—now to be herding sheep on this barren wasteland in the Midianite wilderness. Where are You, God? Why am I here?"

These are the kinds of questions that people ask in every generation. "What am I doing here in this place? My life seems to have no great significance." Every human being born in the image of God has a built-in aspiration for significance. We want our lives to count, for people to say more about us when we die than the dates of our birth and death. We want to leave a legacy that is a benefit to other people, so our lives were worthwhile.

Moses must have asked these questions too, until he saw the bush that was burning but not consumed. God called to him, "Moses, this is holy ground, and I have a holy mission for you." God could have shouted from the heavens and said directly to Pharaoh, "Let My people go." But that's not how God does things; He gave that responsibility to Moses. This was Moses' life's goal, his destiny—that God would work through him to redeem the people of Israel.

We've already seen in this study that God is eternal, and everything that is created by Him has a beginning in time and manifests the attributes of change or mutability. The same God who created the world also engaged with it throughout history, and for all eternity purposed a plan of redemption for His fallen creatures. Moses' meeting with God in the Midianite wilderness had to do not only with creation but also with God's redemptive purposes.

Look again at the discussion that Moses had with God when God revealed Himself by the sacred name:

God said to Moses, "I AM WHO I AM." And he said, "Say this to the people of Israel: 'I AM has sent me to you.'" God also said to Moses, "Say this to the people of Israel: 'The LORD, the God of your fathers, the God of Abraham, the God of Isaac, and the God of Jacob, has sent me to you.' This is my name forever, and thus I am to be remembered throughout all generations. Go and gather the elders of Israel together and say to them, 'The LORD, the God of your fathers, the God of Abraham, of Isaac, and of Jacob, has appeared to me.'" (Ex. 3:14–16)

It's important to see the continuity between the One who is identified as the God of their fathers—the God of Abraham, Isaac, and Jacob—and the One who is now revealing His memorial name, "I AM WHO I AM." Why does God call Himself the God of Abraham, the God of Isaac, and the God of Jacob? And how did the people of Israel get into this situation that God was addressing with Moses? It goes back to Abraham, whom God called out of a land of paganism, idolatry, and darkness. He called him out of Mesopotamia, of Ur of the Chaldeans, and told him to get up and leave the land of his birth: "Go from your country and your kindred and your father's house to the land that I will show you" (Gen. 12:1).

The author of Hebrews wrote that by faith, Abraham

obeyed this mandate from God (Heb. 11:8). You may know how his story unfolded: God promised Abraham a child in his old age—and through this child, the whole universe would be blessed, and the descendants of Abraham would be like the stars of the sky and the sand by the sea. But Abraham didn't live to see that multiplication of his seed. He lived to see the promised son, Isaac, but he never saw the Promised Land. However, at the end of his life, he told Isaac of this promise, and the patriarchal blessing was then transferred from Abraham to Isaac. In like manner, at the end of his life, Isaac gave the patriarchal blessing to Jacob.

In the latter chapters of the book of Genesis, one of the sons of Jacob, Joseph, was betrayed by his brothers, sold into slavery, and then thrown into prison. Because he could interpret dreams, he found favor with the reigning pharaoh—and because of his administrative abilities, Joseph rose to the level of prime minister over all of Egypt. In this role, Joseph was the head of the storehouse enterprise in Egypt. When famine came to the land, the people in Egypt, under Joseph's leadership, were prepared.

The famine also came to the land of Jacob and the brothers of Joseph. Again, you may know how the story went: Jacob sent his sons down to Egypt to get food, and eventually there was a reunion between the other sons of Jacob and

Joseph. Then Jacob and the rest of the family migrated to Egypt, and the land of Goshen was given to them.

That's how the Israelites got to Egypt in the first place—but then we have that ominous report: "Now there arose a new king over Egypt, who did not know Joseph" (Ex. 1:8). Instead of treating the children of Israel as guests in the land with special privileges, Pharaoh enslaved them and used them for hard labor. That's the context: the whole purpose of this meeting between God and Moses was to address the problem of Jewish slavery. God said to Moses, "I have surely seen the affliction of my people who are in Egypt and have heard their cry because of their task-masters. I know their sufferings, and I have come down to deliver them out of the hand of the Egyptians" (Ex. 3:7–8). This was a watershed moment, not only for Israel but for the entire history of the world—because, in that context, God promised redemption and liberation.

The author of the book of Hebrews writes, "Therefore, holy brothers, you who share in a heavenly calling, consider Jesus, the apostle and high priest of our confession, who was faithful to him who appointed him, just as Moses also was faithful in all God's house" (Heb. 3:1–2). In the earlier chapters of the book, the author of Hebrews compares and contrasts Jesus to the angels: "For to which of the angels did God ever say, 'You are my Son, today I have begotten you'? . . . And to which of the angels has he ever said, 'Sit at my right hand until I make your enemies a footstool for your feet'?" (Heb. 1:5, 13). The answer is none, of course. The superiority of Christ to the angels is apparent.

But what comes next is a comparison and contrast between Jesus and Moses. Don't miss the significance of that, because Moses was the mediator of the old covenant. That office made Moses one of the most important and extraordinary people in the whole Old Testament. It was through the mediatorial work of Moses that the nation of Israel was established and that the Ten Commandments were delivered to the people. As a mediator, he stood between God and the people of Israel. Insofar as Moses was the mediator of the old covenant, he foreshadowed the greater Mediator who would come later—the Mediator of the new covenant, Christ Himself.

The New Testament, on one occasion, says there is only one Mediator between God and man, Jesus Christ (1 Tim. 2:5). Here the Apostle Paul means that there is only one supreme Mediator who, in His mediatorial office, brings to the task both His humanity and His deity. Moses could mediate things for the people of Israel as a human being, but not as God incarnate. Yet we read in Hebrews the comparison, affirming that "Moses also was faithful in all God's house" (Heb. 3:2). It continues:

> For Jesus has been counted worthy of more glory than Moses—as much more glory as the builder of a house has more honor than the house itself. (For every house is built by someone, but the builder of all things is God.) Now Moses was faithful in all God's house as a servant, to testify to the things that were to be spoken later, but Christ is faithful over God's house as a son. And we are his house, if indeed we hold fast our confidence and our boasting in our hope. (Heb. 3:3–6)

Moses was faithful as a servant, but he didn't own the house. The house was not built by him; he simply served in it. But in the new covenant, we have a house whose maker and builder is Christ, and that house is His people—we are that house, owned by the Son, who is not a servant but the master of the house. Later, in the famous "Hall of Faith," we read these comments about Moses:

> By faith Moses, when he was born, was hidden for three months by his parents, because they saw

that the child was beautiful, and they were not afraid of the king's edict. By faith Moses, when he was grown up, refused to be called the son of Pharaoh's daughter, choosing rather to be mistreated with the people of God than to enjoy the fleeting pleasures of sin. He considered the reproach of Christ greater wealth than the treasures of Egypt, for he was looking to the reward. By faith he left Egypt, not being afraid of the anger of the king, for he endured as seeing him who is invisible. By faith he kept the Passover and sprinkled the blood, so that the Destroyer of the firstborn might not touch them.

By faith the people crossed the Red Sea as on dry land, but the Egyptians, when they attempted to do the same, were drowned. (Heb. 11:23–29)

This is a saga of the calling of God upon Moses' life. Moses only weakly foreshadows the Mediator of the new covenant, the owner of His house, whose work of liberation and salvation makes the work of Moses pale into insignificance. God addressed Satan through the ministry of His only begotten Son, but the message through the incarnate Word was this: Let My people go. By the word of His power, the greatest exodus in human history took place when Christ freed His saints from the bondage of sin. He has received the reward that He would sit at the right hand of God the Father, demonstrating that His mission far surpassed the mission of Moses. He was the One who was like Moses but greater than Moses, because His work of salvation was the ultimate liberation.

Most of those people who left Egypt under the mandate of God never made it to the Promised Land; in the final analysis, they were faithless. But all whom Jesus redeems make it to the Promised Land. He reserves a place in heaven for them, so that the mediatorial work that He has accomplished cannot be put to shame or left undone. He is the incarnation of "I AM"—in fact, these very words are used throughout the gospel of John. Jesus said: "I am the bread of life" (John 6:48); "I am the light of the world" (John 8:12); "Before Abraham was, I am" (John 8:58); "I am the door. If anyone enters by me, he will be saved and will go in and out and find pasture" (John 10:9); "I am the good shepherd" (John 10:11); "I am the resurrection and the life" (John 11:25); "I am the way, and the truth, and the life" (John 14:6). The very name by which God revealed Himself in that bush is used by the Son of God in His incarnation.

Chapter Ten

A SHADOW
OF CHRIST

It's safe to say that the greatest mission ever accomplished, in the history of the world, is that which was accomplished by the Lord Jesus Christ in the redemption of His people from sin. But the second most important act of redemption ever accomplished in history, and the second most difficult mission ever given by God to a human being, was the mission God gave to Moses. Most Christians are so familiar with the story that they miss the existential agony that Moses went through as the enormity of the task that God set before him struck his consciousness.

After God had revealed to Moses His sacred name, He then said:

Go and gather the elders of Israel together and say to them, "The LORD, the God of your fathers, the God of Abraham, of Isaac, and of Jacob, has appeared to me, saying, 'I have observed you and what has been done to you in Egypt, and I promise that I will bring you up out of the affliction of Egypt to the land of the Canaanites, the Hittites, the Amorites, the Perizzites, the Hivites, and the Jebusites, a land flowing with milk and honey.'" And they will listen to your voice, and you and the elders of Israel shall go to the king of Egypt and say to him, "The LORD, the God of the Hebrews, has met with us; and now, please let us go a three days' journey into the wilderness, that we may sacrifice to the LORD our God." But I know that the king of Egypt will not let you go unless compelled by a mighty hand. So I will stretch out my hand and strike Egypt with all the wonders that I will do in it; after that he will let you go. And I will give this people favor in the sight of the Egyptians; and when you go, you shall not go empty, but each woman shall ask of her neighbor, and any woman who lives in her house, for silver and gold jewelry, and for clothing. You shall put them on your sons and on your daughters. So you shall plunder the Egyptians. (Ex. 3:16–22)

The point of the exodus was not simply to redeem people *from* oppression, but to redeem them *to* something: from slavery to worship. That's true in an even higher manner in the redemptive work of Christ in the New Testament: we are not saved simply because we need to be saved, but so that we might worship Him. That's the point of your salvation—to worship the Lord your God. That's why, for example, the author of Hebrews said we are never to neglect assembling together as saints (Heb. 10:25). We don't come to church just to have our attendance taken; we come to church because the Lord has redeemed us, and the people of God should have their hearts filled with reverence and adoration and should come into the corporate assembly of the people of God to worship Him.

Yet, even after God gave His assurance that He would reveal His power to Pharaoh, Moses might have thought, "Is that all I have to do? I'm going to tell these people that you appeared to me in a burning bush, that they're supposed to follow me on the largest strike in the history of the world against the most powerful king on the face of the globe—and they're going to follow me?" Scripture shows us that Moses struggled with God's instructions: "Then Moses answered, 'But behold, they will not believe me or listen to my voice, for they will say, "The LORD did not appear to you"'" (Ex. 4:1). This is the question that Moses had: How am I ever going to convince anyone, the people of Israel or Pharaoh, that I am speaking Your Word? How can I prove that this message is not something I dreamed up in the heat of the desert, but that I am speaking the unvarnished truth that You gave to me?

Was Moses supposed to say to the people, "That's the experience I had; you have to just take it by faith"? Or, "Pharaoh, you may not believe this, but jump into the abyss in a leap of faith, and perhaps you'll come to the conclusion that indeed the Lord God omnipotent is the author of this message." That's not what God told Moses to do. It's very important to understand how God answered this question:

> The LORD said to him, "What is that in your hand?" He said, "A staff." And he said, "Throw it on the ground." So he threw it on the ground, and it became a serpent, and Moses ran from it. But the LORD said to Moses, "Put out your hand and catch it by the tail"—so he put out his hand

and caught it, and it became a staff in his hand—
"that they may believe that the LORD, the God
of their fathers, the God of Abraham, the God
of Isaac, and the God of Jacob, has appeared to you."
(Ex. 4:2–5)

God caused Moses to turn a stick into a snake so these
people might believe that he was truly communicating
God's word. Sometimes people will say, "If I could just see
a miracle, then that would prove to me that God exists."
But the miracles in the Bible were not given to persuade
people of the existence of God; God's existence had been
established long before there were any kind of episodes of
the miraculous. The purpose of the miracles in the Bible
was to prove the legitimacy and the validity of an agent
of revelation—someone whom God had commissioned to
speak His word. We have a tendency to read the Bible as
if miracles were occurring every other day, to everyone in
history. Actually, a close look at the appearance of miracles
in the Bible reveals that they're clustered. There were miracles that attended Moses in his mediatorial office, but then
very little miraculous activity took place for centuries.

The next redemptive-historical period that had a clus-
ter of miracles was with Elijah. God verified the law, and

then the prophets, through miraculous works. After that, we don't read about miracles from Jonah, Habakkuk, Ezekiel, or any other prophets of the Old Testament, until a blaze of miracles attended the appearance of Jesus. There was a special focal point for the clustering of miracles in biblical history: all of them surrounded the issue of the proclaimed Word of God.

After the first miracle that God gave Moses, he added another:

> Again, the LORD said to him, "Put your hand inside your cloak." And he put his hand inside his cloak, and when he took it out, behold, his hand was leprous like snow. Then God said, "Put your hand back inside your cloak." So he put his hand back inside his cloak, and when he took it out, behold, it was restored like the rest of his flesh. "If they will not believe you," God said, "or listen to the first sign, they may believe the latter sign. If they will not believe even these two signs or listen to your voice, you shall take some water from the Nile and pour it on the dry ground, and the water that you shall take from the Nile will become blood on the dry ground." (Ex. 4:6–9)

This is exactly what happened. Then the series of plagues that fell upon the Egyptians, designed to demonstrate to Pharaoh that Moses was not some dreamer with a crazy vision, but that he spoke the words of the Lord God omnipotent.

Do you know who really understood the principal reason why Jesus did the miracles he did? His name was Nicodemus, and he came to Jesus at night. He said, "Rabbi, we know that you are a teacher come from God, for no one can do these signs that you do unless God is with him" (John 3:2). Beyond that point, the theology of Nicodemus was pretty suspect. But at that moment, his theology was absolutely sound—so much more than the enemies of Jesus, like Nicodemus' fellow Pharisees, who didn't deny the miracles of Christ but who came perilously close to blasphemy against the Holy Spirit when they attributed the power of Jesus' miracles not to God but to Satan.

Satan cannot perform miracles. The Bible warns us against the signs that Satan will perform, deceiving even the elect; but those signs are described as lying signs and wonders. That doesn't mean that they are true miracles that are performed for satanic purposes. Rather, they are false signs or tricks; they might be more astonishing than the most impressive magic acts, but they are still tricks. Satan is not God. He cannot do the things that God can do. Real miracles that authenticate God's messengers are acts that only God can do, such as creating something out of nothing or raising people from the dead. Satan can't control the laws of nature; he's just a magician. He's good at his craft, but his craft is altogether evil.

We see how that took place in the confrontation that Moses had with the magicians of Pharaoh's court (Ex. 7:10–13). Moses took that rod, threw it on the ground, and it turned into a snake. But the magicians of Pharaoh just yawned and threw their sticks on the floor too—and they all became snakes. It was the oldest trick in the history of sleight-of-hand: inside each of their sticks was a snake. The sticks collapsed, so the snakes that were already in there could come out. Pharaoh's court thought that was all Moses was doing, too. But Moses' "trick" was real; his snake ate all of their snakes. Those magicians were no match for Moses—because they were no match for God. All the trickery and machinations that Pharaoh's court magicians had could not really turn the Nile into blood or bring about the plagues. They certainly did not have the power of the Passover.

The miracles in the New Testament had an immediate

purpose: healing people who were sick, raising people from the dead, ministering to suffering, and many other acts of compassion. But in the final analysis, those miracles authenticated and validated that Jesus was and is the Word of God, that Jesus spoke the truth. Likewise, in the burning bush we see the revelation of the person of God, of the power of God, and of the eternality of God. We see the revelation of the compassion of God, the redemption of God, and now, finally, the truth of God.

NOTES

Chapter Eight

1   Richard Carrier, "Antony Flew Considers God . . . Sort Of," *The Secular Web,* archived from the original on May 21, 2014.

2   Bertrand Russell, *Why I Am Not a Christian, and Other Essays on Religion and Related Subjects* (New York: Touchstone, 1957), 6.

ABOUT THE AUTHOR

Dr. R.C. Sproul (1939–2017) was founder of Ligonier Ministries, founding pastor of Saint Andrew's Chapel in Sanford, Fla., first president of Reformation Bible College, and executive editor of *Tabletalk* magazine. He was recognized throughout the world for his articulate defense of the inerrancy of Scripture and the need for God's people to stand with conviction upon His Word. His radio program, *Renewing Your Mind*, is still broadcast daily on hundreds of radio stations around the world and can also be heard online. He was author of more than one hundred books, including *The Holiness of God*, *Chosen by God*, *Faith Alone*, and *Everyone's a Theologian*. He also served as general editor of the *Reformation Study Bible* and wrote several children's books, including *The Donkey Who Carried a King* and *The Knight's Map*.